# Vital Signs

## from five concerned poets

Dave Cavanagh, Gail Holst-Warhaft,
Marjorie Maddox, Tony Magistrale,
Sharon Webster

I consider poetry a source of innocence
full of revolutionary forces. It is my
mission to direct those forces against a
world my conscience cannot accept...

--Odysseus Elytis

Fomite
Burlingon, VT
fomitepress.com

5-10-2025

Tony Magistrale

**Heads Down**

In the summer, between high school and
college,
I worked for my father in downtown Buffalo

shuffling important legal papers from
inside one skyscraper to another,

like a board game that had no ending
and many rules I never wanted to understand.
On the thirtieth floor of one of these buildings,

Liberty Insurance Company owned an entire
open space.
The elevator would open to reveal

hundreds of seated female secretaries aligned in
perfectly straight rows,

heads down, typing on typewriters
(there were no computers)
that clacked and clacked
accumulating into a steady drone.
I used to wonder
how they could abide,

minute after minute, hour after hour,
the ceaseless cacophony of American business.

I would imagine them sometimes,
in a fit of morbidity,
arranged as future tombstones in grey
solemnity, row upon row, stretching to the
horizon,
each one bearing the same epitaph:

*I clacked until I could clack no longer.*

On other occasions,
I would recognize Henry David Thoreau,
the only male among this sea of working
women,
standing in an aisle alongside
desks and typewriters

      his face contorted and distressed,
      his eyes tracking the movement of a
minute hand
      as it climbed a wall clock's numbers
      in the front of the room

towards eternity.

Marjorie Maddox

**True or False**

By sentence end, *isn't* becomes *is*,
the dictionary shredded at the door.
The liar claims reality as his.

The very stable genius, who's a whiz
at contradictions, apparently abhors
sentences. Becoming what he isn't is

the logophile's goal. Rise up, resist
prevarications. Cease this civil war.
The liar claims reality as his.

More Truth Social: the deeper the abyss.
Thesaurus, grammar, spelling—out the door;
the end of sense when *isn't* becomes *is*.

Pharaoh of phonies—despot of the biz,
the "educated" clapping, wanting more.
By sentence end, *isn't* becomes *is*.
The liar claims reality as his.

## Epiphany

January 6, 2021

And so they rush the steps and bash the doors.
With windows smashed, the winter light breaks
    in.
Forgotten is the frankincense, the myrrh,
the gold the wisemen brought. Instead, our kin

or neighbors storm the halls. We recognize
their faces, tense with hate. In different form
they look a bit like us. Yet we surmise
this mob that waves its flags, together swarms

toward House or Senate, cannot live so near.
We say hello on walks? They guard our homes?
This is the hard epiphany we fear:
the ones we loathe and love might be the same.

And that bright star? We find the manger bare
except for all our anger swaddled there.

The poem "Epiphany" is reprinted by permission
from the 24 February 2021 issue of *Christian Century*;
reprinted in *Verse Virtual* and *Begin with a Question*
(Paraclete Press, 2022).

**In the post-apocalyptic polls,**

the list is long and bloodied
and every name is his.

Still, the undead, winding their way
around an abandoned KFC

and two downed replicas of Air Force One,
raise any loosely hanging limb

in protest. With placards held high,
by midnight they shuffle-jerk

their gashed hips and brain-
spilling skulls past the stained

electoral maps of Fox and CNN, then
groan and moan their prophecies

of us, who are just now opening
a blind eye, just now twitching

middle fingers, our gaping mouths
ravenous to join them.

"In the post-apocalyptic polls," was previously
published in *White Stag Journal* and is reprinted by
permission of the author, who owns all rights.

## Cold Front

Gray and heavy doesn't cut it,
but can't you see Sky's fists pushing down on us
squeezing subservient henchmen as low and hard
as he dares without breaking word with the local
weatherman, who's also tight in his grip—no sense pretending
otherwise. He's already kidnapped the wife's howl, replayed it
whenever the loser's late on rainy day payments for hot tips,
cool predictions, or whatever's really coming up the coast
in time for tourist season. It's all worth a pretty penny
to not rough up the pines, pummel the horizon enough
to bruise even the shadows of light oozing out like an
unrequited cry for help. The warning before
the warning still goes by the nickname Stormy,
putting up a good front for other heavy hitters,
swearing his mantras of *local loyalty*, *family first*.
until he doesn't, one catastrophic costly rampage
after another freezing out even the most familiar
and familial trusts, only those in the center
of his far-reaching eye somewhat safe from all-out
chaos, utter destruction that somehow keeps
crowning him, and all his windy surrogates,
boss man/mafia king, don.

Sharon Webster

## Sentinels

I'm giving myself
this day of remembrance,
this holy day of forgetting. The song,

*Pressure Drop*, plays
over and over
in my head. There
is my first vivid memory:

I'm three years old
on top of a sandy embankment
watching the waves
at my feet, saying,
out loud and triumphant, "They can't get me
          from here."
There is no way around it.
Some things were hard. When my mother
drove her car into the Ohio River it was
devastating,

but triumphant
too. So decisive
for a woman who, at the time
was unsure
of everything.
Everything:  frozen peas,
frozen carrots
or whether to continue
living. But the thing is
you couldn't blame her.
The way things were, no choice
looked that good.

And the water was shallow

where she went in.
and it was the heart of town
with people around. So maybe,
as the wife of a mayor, what she did
was closer to performance art,
to say fuck all this,
precise
eloquent. Who knows?
But when I found out last winter
that Lizzie tried to kill herself
when the bombs
were dropping
and the temperature
wouldn't go
above zero, after

the comforting words I said
Adrienne Rich's words:
"Every woman's death diminishes
me." "Yeah,"
Lizzie said, "but
they enrich me too."

I didn't know
what she meant
then, but now I think maybe
she meant the spirits

of those women stay
on as sentinels

to warn us. Snagged
on human
terrain during
their violent passage. Stay

on as ghosts

who say: Not
this way. Turn back.
Not. Not. Not.
Pay attention
to what isn't

whole yet. I am watching the waves
fold into themselves.
I am saying, slowly
and without words,
"They can't get me from here."

## Living Here

Outside, we walk
into the unsuspecting night.
The sky
is stiff as slate. Late
there's a moon. We stare at the edges
until our hearts break down.


      ii
The trees are jet black
roots in reverse,
still as statues.
Are they going to speak?
They stand so still.
What do they seek?
Are they envoys from a world
we don't understand?
When we stop walking
they flood the sky with grief.


      iii
The air is glass.
These nights the trees
have no tongues:
nothing warm.
The only sounds
are those of warning.

We haven't left yet.

## The Broken Church

I walk beside the shuttered church. It's hot
and July. There's Covid. The homeless people
are large purple shadows under the trees.
The quiet breaks
into two demolition
crews across the street. Huge
rusted shovels
eat the dirt and grab
at the hole. The groaning
groans on. Many trucks
hide behind shabby walls, disembodied,
        so many
unsheltered humans
asleep in shadows
at noon under jackets
at peace for now
or at least
in place. I keep walking, careful
not to intrude, my footsteps
quiet with them, blessing
them.

Gail Holst-Warhaft

## Eyeless in Gaza

### Eyeless

*Promise was that I*
*Should Israel from Philistian yoke deliver*
*Ask for this great deliverer now, and find him*
*Eyeless in Gaza at the Mill with slaves ...*
John Milton, *Samson Agonistes*

Pin-up boy of the Israelites
Samson was undone by a woman.
Delilah was pretty, maybe
a whore or just short of money--
she was promised a whole lot.
Samson, they knew, had a weakness
for women. It took her a while
but finally he told her his secret.

As they shaved off his hair she took
a handful. It was long and black
as night and it smelled of cloves.
She would bury her fingers in it
when they made love.

They never told her they would take
 his eyes too. His screams sent her mad.
She threw the money they paid her at their
feet.

His eyes gouged out he was kept
a slave with other slaves
grinding grain in the mill
but as he ground grain
his hair began to grow.
They forced him to show off his strength

12

in the arena, but he pretended to rest
and grasped two marble columns,
bringing the roof down on the Philistines
and himself, crushing them all like grain.


## In Gaza

*But I will send a fire on the wall of Gaza, which
shall devour the palaces thereof.*

Amos, (1)


My home was water boiling
on the blue eye of the stove,
the children playing, shouting,
little Ahmet crying
till his lips clamped my breast,
Umm Kalthoum on the radio,
a melon yellow as the sun
sliced open on the table.

My home got used to the sounds
of war – thud of bombs
whine of shells, thunder
of buildings falling. And sights
repeated day after day.
Men with dead children
In their arms, women digging
through rubble till their fingers bleed,
lines of people fleeing,
unsteady loads strapped
on donkeys, children too frightened
to cry, women weeping
old men weeping,
warriors weeping, the terrible
silence before the weeping.

In the dreadful dark of Gaza's night
who is the deliverer, who the devourer?

Climb onto the roof of a building
 that still stands; look down on the rubble
 that was once a city, see it laid out
like a gutted fish. Who is the deliverer?
Who the devourer?

We who wanted to live our lives
have become scraps of his feast --
bones, offal, tufts of hair.

By the candle we saved we see
empty beds, a bare table.
We have no homes to return to.


**Olives**

All you have to do to make the sights
and sounds of war disappear is press a button.
One minute they are in your room, the next
they are gone, back to where they came from,
to that strip of land like a dog's bone
squeezed between the sea and the invaders.

In the dark that is Gaza, if anything survives
it will be olive trees that can manage
without water for a year or two.
Open your eyes just long enough
to see green fruit under silver leaves,
a farmer dipping his finger in oil.

He tastes the sun, the ochre earth
that lies on his ancestors, cousins, children.
They've bull-dozed his orchards, his lemons,

pomegranates. The few trees still alive
bear bitter fruit. The farmer
may not survive but the olives, the olives…


## A Wrathful God

*What in me is dark*
*Illumine, what is low raise and support…*
                    *John Milton. Paradise Lost*

Blind, he had a vision of Paradise to finish.
He tried to justify heaven's vengeance
but Milton couldn't stop his villain,
banished to eternal darkness and chained
on a burning lake, from stealing the limelight.

And why were the first couple driven
out of Paradise? Was Eve's curiosity
crime enough to curse a race?
Was her failure to resist temptation,
like Pandora's, the cause of human misery?

Milton knew it would take great skill
to justify the vengeance of a wrathful god
 to his readers. He left two poems behind.
*Paradise Lost* was his masterpiece.
Does anyone still read *Paradise Regained*?

**Money Talks**

*I live with you. You think about me all the time. I
seldom think of you.*

*You made me. You wanted me and you made me.*

*I started out a useful tool. Helped you trade goods,
pleasantries, trust. I brought home the bacon.*

*Your rich imagination – that's where I came from.
But now you only imagine getting rich.*

*You've dirtied me. You've lied and raped and killed for me.*

*You've laundered me. A lot of me hides in offshore
accounts. Just like your days, they're numbered.*

*I once was bullion. Then coin. Then paper. Then
plastic.*

*Then pixel. I'm more and more cryptic.*

*I used to sit snug in your wallet. Now I never know
where I am, what I am.*

*I get more and more remote. Or is that you?
An object of desire. A power play. A starch for ego.
That's what I am to you.*

*What will you not do for me? Almost nothing. But
not for me. For you. Always just for you.*

*Sometimes I think I'm going out of fashion. I've lost
currency.*

*But no, there you are again, grasping. You want to have your way with me.*

*You keep careful ledgers of my movements. You count and count me. I can't count on you. You're drunk on me. I'm wasted.*

*I keep you awake at night. But you're no fun anymore. If it's not worry, it's scheming. If not scheming, fawning. I hate fawning.*

*No matter how much of me you possess, you feel poor.*

*You can never get enough of me.*

*You move as if you're in control, but in the backroom of your psyche you shiver. Your days are a tight tourniquet. You shoot up dollar lust.*

*You think you're buying time with me, but really you're selling it. Either way, you're running low.*

## January 6, Feast of the Epiphany

The MAGi stormed the stable with their unbelief.
They said they'd followed a star. The animals
and shepherds hid in the stalls. Jesus wailed
and wailed. He was a newborn, after all.

His Father was a no-show, as usual.
Mom was scared but stood her ground.
She held the child, glared at the wise guys.
Joe the carpenter said little. It wasn't his time

yet. The wise guys crashed about. Made
quite a racket. The stable walls shook.
The wise guys yelled a lot, smashed the manger,
waved flags and smelly stuff they'd brought.

They said it was a gift, ha ha. Things got nasty.
Lots of the animals and shepherds were hurt.
Jesus kept crying, only now he had company.
All the animals. After a long while the wise guys

were pushed back, forced out of the stable.
The animals and shepherds returned to grazing,
sleeping, gathering, but something seemed off,
not right. It came to them, an epiphany, things

could never be as they were. Some essence
altered. The only hope -- make a holy day
not to forget, make a promise, repair the stable,
care for the child, watch out for wise guys,pray.

## Nuclear Football
*…the nickname for the 45-pound briefcase that*
*accompanies the U.S President at all times when*
*away from a command center.*

Only the President can put the ball in play.
Carries a laminated ID card with codes
to verify that he (or someday she) is
quarterback supreme. The card is known
as "the biscuit." Once Clinton misplaced
the biscuit for months. When Reagan was shot
and rushed into surgery, the biscuit turned up
later in his shoe on the floor of the ER.
Most of the time the football gets carried
by an officer with top security clearance
called "Yankee White." At the White House,
the President has the Oval Office,
the Resolute Desk, the Situation Room.
The nuclear football is tucked away. Is it
coincidence that a football is oval?
That football is the U.S.'s most popular sport?
That the teams line up against each other
like armies crouched for an attack? If
the President is resolute, if he makes the call,
who will be able to call timeout? Who will
know until there's no more point in knowing
of the Hail Mary launch into the end zone?

## Blue Plastic Radio

He is slumped, a melted bottle shape.
Clutches a blue plastic radio, sinks
day by day into the sidewalk he lives on.

He holds it like an orphan's hand,
holds it like a man who needs
to hold an orphan's hand.

Holds it like it's a savior come too late.
Holds it like a shriek, like a memory,
like a mickey. Holds it like he has forgotten

he is holding it, and he holds it
like a rusted stiff old vice.
No tiny tune from it, no wild rhythm.

No sound at all from the radio
he holds onto like everything
he may have once imagined.

Except an outstretched cup.
He does not hold it like a cup
and he does not look up for pity

or any easy coin. Hunches over it,
head tucked away from the crowd
that tries and tries not to look at him.

Fist and a silent blue radio held
like a talisman, a shield, a signature,
an unopened letter.

**The Recycle Man**

Every groove in the sidewalk announces his
passing. The clatter of a shopping cart bulging
with black trash bags of returnables hanging
over the sides – beer, soda (5 cents each), the
occasional whisky or gin bottle (15 cents!).  At
least twice a day he rattles by in red gym pants
and ball cap, arms out straight in front of him,
leaning into the push, the pace barely slowed
by his loud, sticky load.

He covers miles around town, but our street is
home ground. Home? He hails from Vietnam,
has little English, as I learn one day when I put
out my leavings just as he passes. "Vietnam –
no money," he explains, repeats. After weeks of
unseen exchanges, we're happy to meet face to
face. We labor over words but gladly connect
with eyes, broken phrases. He lives down the
block with his sister and ailing mother. Who
knows what troubles they've fled, the struggles
they grapple with now? He is undaunted. Day
after day he clacks by, stoops for the leftovers
of privilege. Against mean odds, his care, his
cheer, his forward lean as he carts our empties
to the redemption center.

I give him beer cans; he gives me his creased
smile with all that lives within it. His hands
come together with a slight bow of thanks.
I smile and bow awkwardly back. I hope he
knows I owe him.

## To the Person Who Broke into My Car
## Last Night

Strange, I think, the driver's seat pushed way back.
And empty the little bin where I stockpile quarters
for parking. Then it dawns. I must have left
the doors unlocked. You must have sat here,
where I'm sitting. You must be tall.
Thank you for not trashing the glove box
you shuffled through. Or anything, really.
Just a few things moved about here or there.
How long did you sit here, checking nooks
and crannies for cash or whatever's sellable,
just as I am now for what's missing?
Not long, I suppose, but who knows,
maybe you stretched back and relaxed,
leaned into the headrest, or stared through
the windshield to the lamplit street,
savored the dark quiet of your moment,
took some time to think. About what, I wonder?
No surprise you made off with the umbrella.
It was a wet night, wet and cold.

## Laughter in the Time of Covid

I'm laughing so hard I start coughing.
*What did the frog say to the saucepan?*
*You're not so hot.*

I always wanted to be funny. Funny how
things turn out. The kid standing tall
on an electric skateboard looks funny,
like Jesus on water or Leonard DiCaprio
at the prow of the Titanic. The boy's on a roll
with a black mask over nose and mouth.
He looks like Zorro with a clothing failure.
If you're on the far-right side of things
you tend to jam together at gatherings.
If on the left, you keep your distance.
*How do you take an election poll?*
*You ask where people stand.*

If heat kills Covid, the west should be
all better. This year it's pretty much
on fire. Wild! The blue states turned
flame red. Meanwhile, some reds
are turning blue, or at least purple.
Must be hard to breathe there.
Politics are funny, but get too close,
your sense of humor shrivels, like when
taste buds go dead, or smell shuts down.
Just about everybody is some kind of blue
these days, even if they don't notice.

*What did the worker say to the billionaire?*
*It only hurts when I try to eat.*
*What did the eight billion say to the planet?*
*You're not so hot.*
*What did the planet say to the eight billion?*
*How's the breathing going?*
It said,
*There may not be much left to laugh about.*

23

It said,
*You ain't seen nothin' yet.*
And the planet said,
*Nothin' is no laughing matter.*

## I can't breathe

says the black man dying on the street.

I can't breathe,
says the Covid patient, gasping, beat.

I can't breathe,
says the body politic, choking on tweets.

I can't breathe,
says the planet. The stifling heat!

# The Poets

Dave Cavanagh has five books of poems in print. His work has also appeared in numerous journals and anthologies in the U.S., Canada, and Europe. A retired college educator, he lives in Burlington, Vermont, and is an avid (some would say obsessive) cyclist..

Gail Holst-Warhaft is a writer and translator. She has published two collections of her own poetry, *Penelope's Confession and Lucky Country* and translated many of Greece's leading poets and prose-writers.

Marjorie Maddox is a Professor Emerita of English at the Lock Haven campus of Commonwealth University, She has published 17 collections of poetry—including *How Can I Look It Up When I Don't Know How It's Spelled? Spelling Mnemonics and Grammar Tricks* (Kelsay Books), *Seeing Things* (Wildhouse), and *Hover Here* (Broadstone, forthcoming), as well as the ekphrastic collaborations *Small Earthly Space; Heart Speaks, Is Spoken For* (both with Karen Elias) and *In the Museum of My Daughter's Mind* (with daughter Anna Lee Hafer www.hafer.work, a 2023 Dragonfly Book Award in photography/fine arts and American Fiction Winner Award in poetry) and others. Maddox also has published the story collection *What She Was Saying* (Fomite), 4 children's books, and the anthologies *Common Wealth: Contemporary Poets on Pennsylvania* and the forthcoming *Keystone Poetry* (co-editor with Jerry Wemple, PSU Press). Assistant editor of

*Presence*, she hosts Poetry Moment for WPSU-FM.

Tony Magistrale is Professor of English at the University of Vermont. He has published his poetry in *The Harvard Review, The Green Mountains Review, Spillway, Common Ground Review, The Alaska Quarterly Review, Blueline Magazine, Northern New England Review, Literary Laundry, The Dalhouise Review, The Salon, and The Montucky Review*, among other places.

Sharon Webster is a visual artist and a poet. She lives in Burlington, VT and was born in Carrollton, Kentucky. She is a teacher and a caregiver with adults with cognitive challenges.

www.ingramcontent.com/pod-product-compliance
Lightning Source LLC
Chambersburg PA
CBHW021006150626
46549CB00012BA/1373